Doctor Mozart® Music Theory

In-Depth Piano Theory Fun for Music Lessons and Home Schooling

Level 2A – Contents

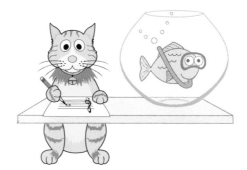

Highly Effective for Beginners Learning a Musical Instrument.

Doctor Mozart workbooks are filled with friendly cartoon characters. They make it fun to learn music theory in-depth. And in-depth music theory knowledge is essential for children learning a musical instrument. Use Doctor Mozart workbooks by themselves or with other teaching materials. Use them for music lessons and for home schooling.

The authors, Machiko and Paul Musgrave, are both graduates of Juilliard. Machiko has taught piano and theory at Soai University in Japan. Paul is an Associate of the Royal Conservatory of Music. The authors hope you enjoy using this book!

Many thanks to Kevin Musgrave for his meticulous proof-reading and insightful suggestions.
Created by Machiko and Paul Christopher Musgrave. Illustrated by Machiko Yamane Musgrave.   1.1.1

Doctor Mozart Music Theory Workbook, Level 2A.   © MMVIII, MMXV Machiko and Paul Christopher Musgrave.   Published by April Avenue Music.   www.DoctorMozart.com

Grand Staff Notes
Review

Write the words and sentences that can help you remember the grand staff note names.

F
D
B
G
Elephants

Line notes

A
F
D
B
Great

Trace.

Space notes

G for _____

F

D for _____

B for _____

All

F for _____

Hint: Elephants Got Big Dirty Feet. FACE. Great Big Dogs Fight Animals. All Cows Eat Grass. Foot, Bubble, Drip, Giraffe.

Make a grand staff. Write all the white key space notes.

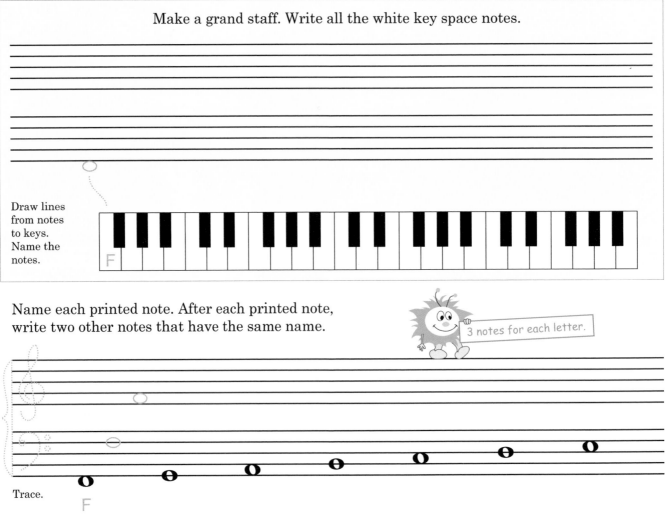

Draw lines from notes to keys. Name the notes.

F

Name each printed note. After each printed note, write two other notes that have the same name.

3 notes for each letter.

Trace.

F

Write the correct clef on each staff.

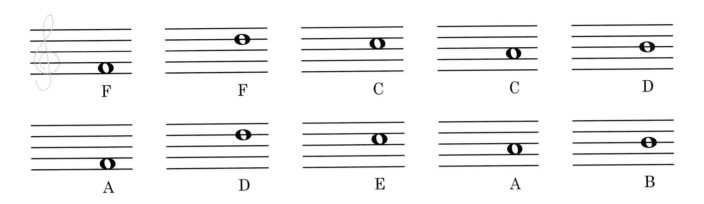

F   F   C   C   D

A   D   E   A   B

Always start by making a grand staff.

After each printed note, write a note in the bass staff that looks similar. Name the notes.

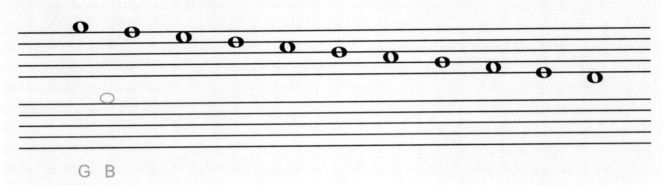

G B

Write 4 different F sharps, 4 G flats, and 3 C sharps.

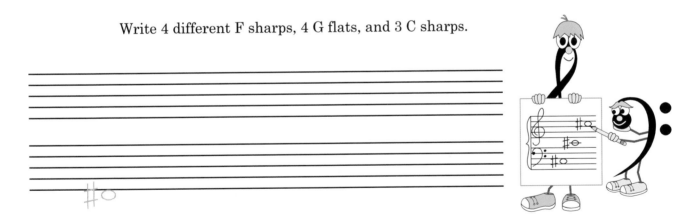

Below, if the red arrow points *up*, write a note that is one semitone *above* the given note.
If the red arrow points *down*, write a note that is one semitone *below* the given note.

Grand Staff & Accidentals

Name the notes.

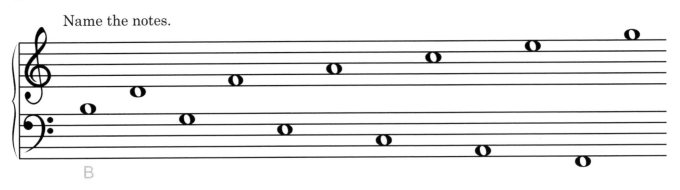

B

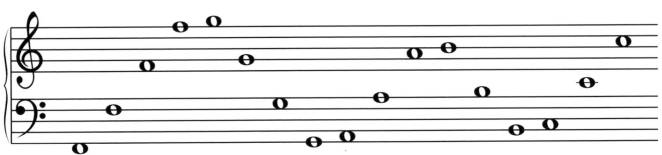

Draw lines from notes to keys.

Accidentals

Sharp Not sharp Sharp Not sharp

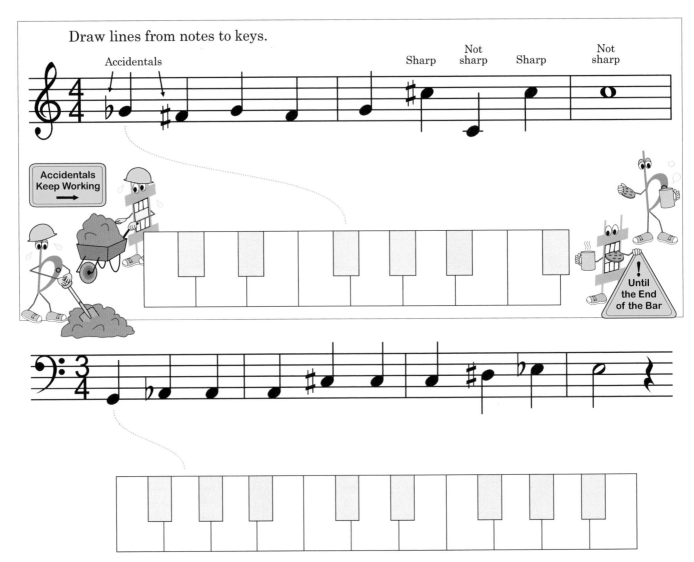

Accidentals Keep Working →

Until the End of the Bar

What are Ledger Notes?

Some notes are too high
or low for the staff.
To write these notes,
we need ledger lines.

Draw lines from notes to keys.
Name the notes on the keyboard.

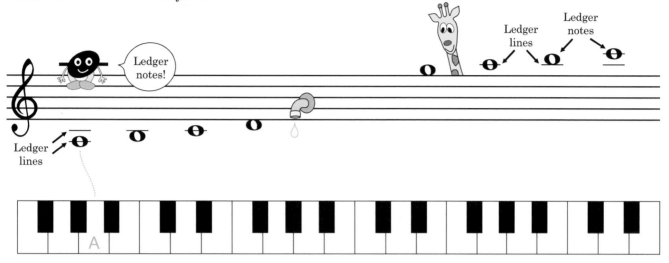

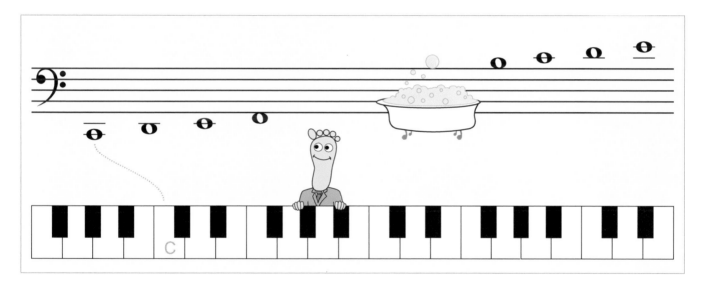

Below, two notes are marked with a red X.
This is because they each have an extra ledger line.
Write an X at any similar mistakes you find.

Ledger lines and staff
lines should be
the same distance apart.

Do not write
this line.

Do not
write this line.

Trace only the correct notes.

Write some ledger notes on your own.

Doctor Mozart Music Theory Workbook, Level 2A.   © MMVIII, MMXV Machiko and Paul Christopher Musgrave.   Published by April Avenue Music.   www.DoctorMozart.com

Treble Staff Ledger Notes

Name these notes.

Ledger

Trace and name.

Write a note at the end of each line. Name each note.

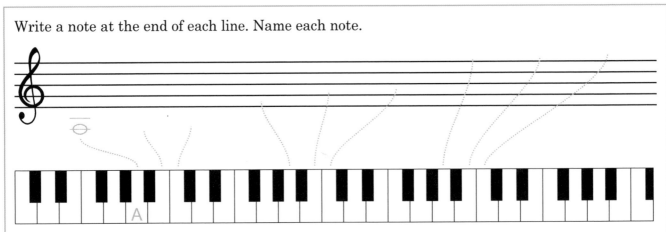

Draw lines from notes to keys.

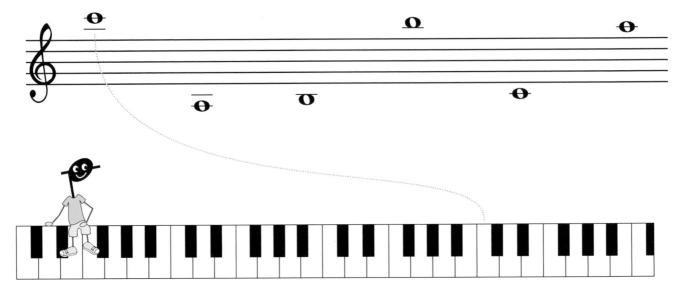

Name the notes.

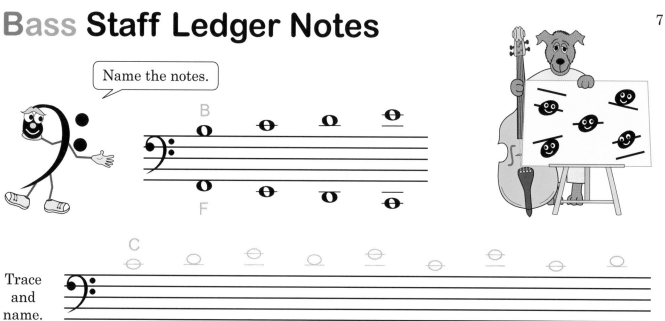

Trace and name.

Write a note at the end of each line. Name each note.

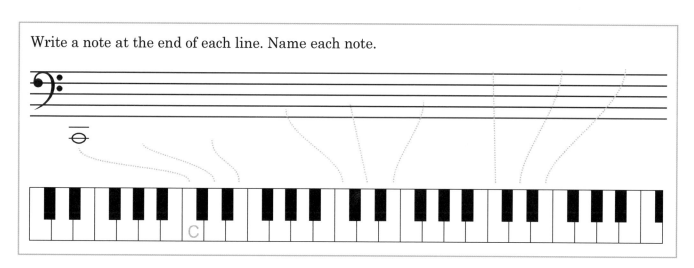

Draw lines from notes to keys.

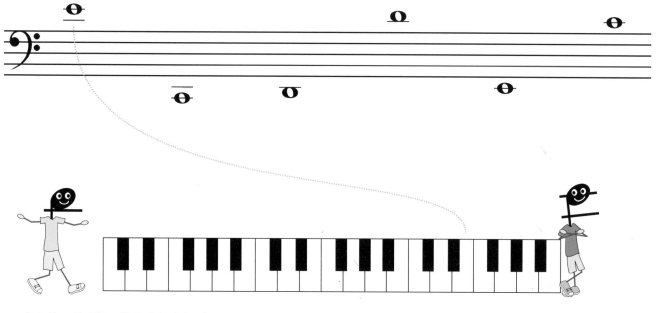

Doctor Mozart Music Theory Workbook, Level 2A.   © MMVIII, MMXV Machiko and Paul Christopher Musgrave.   Published by April Avenue Music.   www.DoctorMozart.com

Ledger Note EXERCISE

Write a note for each letter. If the arrow points up, write the note *above* the staff. If the arrow points down, write the note *below* the staff.

C↑ A↓ B↓ B↑ A↑ C↓   C↑ E↑ D↑ D↓ E↓ C↓

Next, trace and name each note. Draw lines from notes to keys.

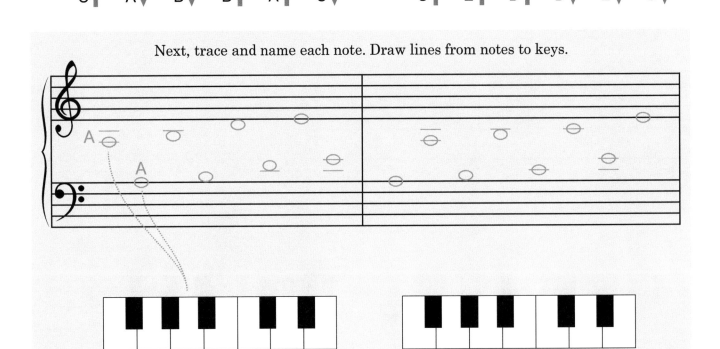

Next, write 6 different ledger notes. Name them.

Draw lines from notes to keys.

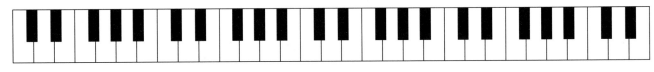

Doctor Mozart Music Theory Workbook, Level 2A. © MMVIII, MMXV Machiko and Paul Christopher Musgrave. Published by April Avenue Music. www.DoctorMozart.com

Musical Sign Quiz

Draw lines to match each sign with its name and meaning.

Signs	Names	Meanings
mp	Mezzo Forte	Quiet
mf	Piano	Louder than *p*
p	Mezzo Piano	A little louder than *mp*
(accent note)	Accent	Play the note one half-step up
♯	Sharp	Play the note loudly
(crescendo)	Tie	Play the first note and hold through the second
(bass clef notes)	Diminuendo	Gradually quieter
♮	Crescendo	Cancel sharps or flats
(diminuendo)	Natural	Gradually louder
♭	Flat	Play the note one half-step down
ff	Fortissimo	Let go of the note immediately
f	Forte	Very loud
(staccato note)	Staccato	Loud
(treble clef notes)	Pianissimo	Play legato
pp	Slur	Very quiet

From Level 1

Doctor Mozart Music Theory Workbook, Level 2A.   © MMVIII, MMXV Machiko and Paul Christopher Musgrave.   Published by April Avenue Music.   www.DoctorMozart.com

Time *Signature*

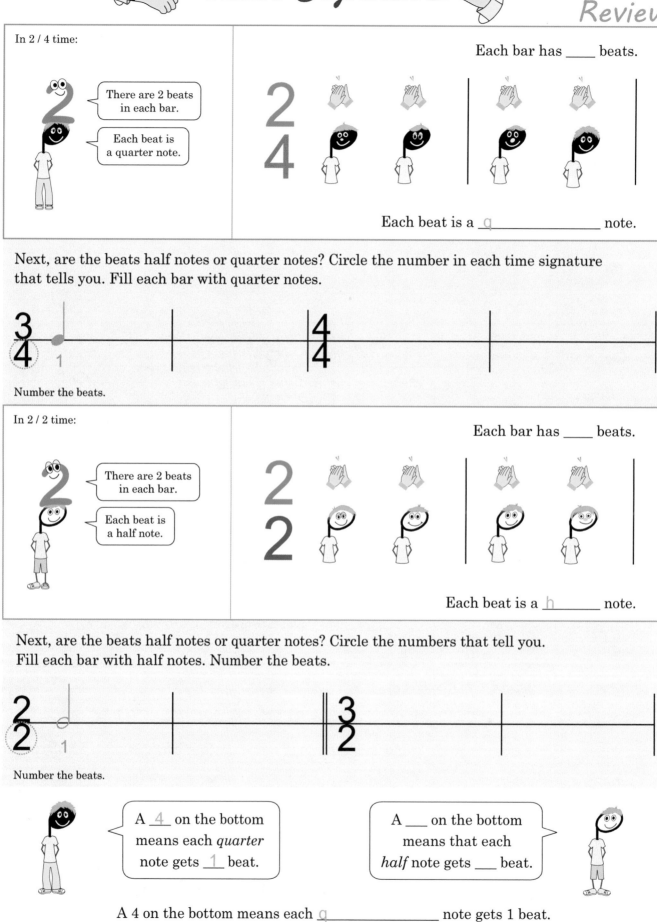

In 2 / 4 time:

There are 2 beats in each bar.

Each beat is a quarter note.

Each bar has ____ beats.

Each beat is a __q_____ note.

Next, are the beats half notes or quarter notes? Circle the number in each time signature that tells you. Fill each bar with quarter notes.

Number the beats.

In 2 / 2 time:

There are 2 beats in each bar.

Each beat is a half note.

Each bar has ____ beats.

Each beat is a __h_____ note.

Next, are the beats half notes or quarter notes? Circle the numbers that tell you.
Fill each bar with half notes. Number the beats.

Number the beats.

A __4__ on the bottom means each *quarter* note gets __1__ beat.

A ____ on the bottom means that each *half* note gets ___ beat.

A 4 on the bottom means each __q_____ note gets 1 beat.

Steady Beats

Accent the first beat in each bar.
Number the beats.

Write an ampersand (&) under any notes that are between the beats.

Tap and count.

Fill each bar with *quarter* notes. Number the beats. Accent the first beat of each bar.

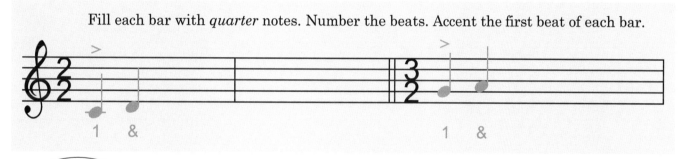

Beats can help fishermen row their boats together.

$\frac{3}{2}$ means 3 ___h___ note beats in each bar.

$\frac{3}{4}$ means 3 _____ note beats in each bar.

$\frac{2}{2}$ means 2 _____ note beats in each bar.

$\frac{2}{4}$ means 2 _____ note beats in each bar.

Write an X under any bar that has the wrong number of beats.

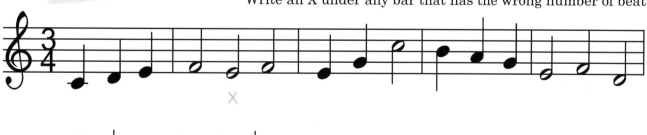

Doctor Mozart Music Theory Workbook, Level 2A.   © MMVIII, MMXV Machiko and Paul Christopher Musgrave.   Published by April Avenue Music.   www.DoctorMozart.com

LEDGER *Note Quiz*

Fill both the treble and bass staffs
with quarter, half, and whole notes.

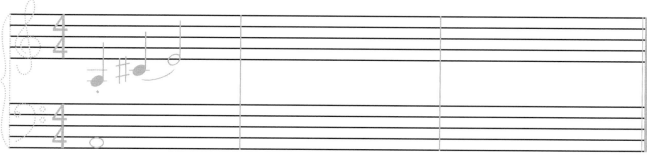

Number
the beats.

1

Include some ledger notes, slurs, ties, accents, accidentals, and staccato quarter notes.

Make a grand staff. Write a 2 / 2 time signature. Then do the same as above.

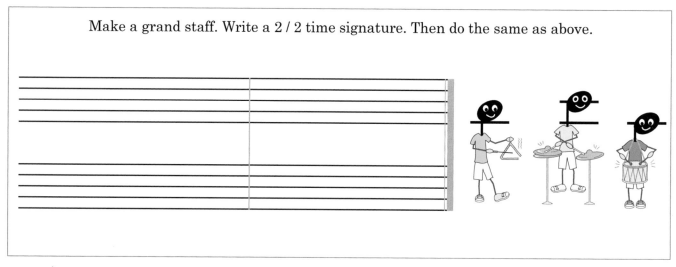

Fill
in the
blanks.

$\frac{2}{2}$ means there are _____ _____ note beats in each bar.

$\frac{3}{2}$ means there are _____ _____ note beats in each bar.

Write 6 different ledger notes. Include some accidentals. Draw lines from notes to keys.

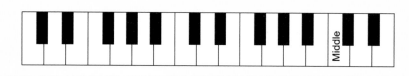

Middle

Doctor Mozart Music Theory Workbook, Level 2A.   © MMVIII, MMXV Machiko and Paul Christopher Musgrave.   Published by April Avenue Music.   www.DoctorMozart.com

Ledger Note FUN

Write 6 different ledger notes: 3 above the staff, and 3 below. Include some accidentals.

Draw lines.

Make a grand staff. Write any 10 notes you like, but include 5 different C sharps.

Draw lines.

Make a grand staff. Near middle C, write a note for each letter – two different ways.

A   B   C   D   E

What is Half of a Half Note?

If you want to share a muffin equally with a friend, cut it into two equal pieces.

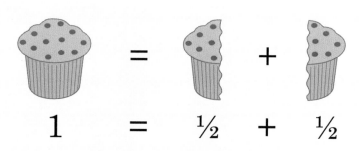

Then you can eat half the muffin and your friend can eat the other half.

$$1 = \frac{1}{2} + \frac{1}{2}$$

The word *half* is also written as ½.

Answer with a note:

How many quarter note beats? Write a number:

What kind of note is half as long as a *whole* note?

1 whole note = 1 half note + ____ half note.

Write a + and = sign to complete the equation.

A half note is __h____ as long as a whole note.

What kind of note is half as long as a *half* note?

1 half note = ____ quarter note + ____ quarter note.

Write a + and = sign to complete the equation.

A quarter note is __h____ as long as a half note.

Doctor Mozart Music Theory Workbook, Level 2A.   © MMVIII, MMXV Machiko and Paul Christopher Musgrave.   Published by April Avenue Music.   www.DoctorMozart.com

Staccato & Dotted Notes

Staccato notes and *dotted* notes are not the same.

If you see a dot *above* or *below* a note, like this ♩ then the note is **staccato**.

Let go of that note immediately after you play it.

A note is _____ if there is a dot above or below it.

Let go of that note _____ after you play it.

If you see a dot *after* a note like this ♩. then the note is *not* staccato. Instead, it is called a **dotted note**. It should be held *longer*.

A dotted note should be held _____.

Below, circle the notes that should be held longer.

Trace the gray dotted half notes.

When the note head is on a *space*, the dot should be written in the *same* space.

When the note head is on a *line*, the dot should be written in the space *above*.

For each letter below, write a dotted half note. If you see an arrow pointing up, write the note above the staff. If you see an arrow pointing down, write the note below the staff.

A   D↑   F   C↑   G   C↓   D↓   D   C

Dotted Half Note Chocolate

Half Note Henry   Quarter Note Quincy   Dotted Half Note Doreen

Henry can eat ___ pieces of chocolate. Quincy can eat ___. Doreen can eat ___.

Draw the chocolate squares.

[ ]   +   =

Henry's chocolate   Half of Henry's chocolate   Doreen's chocolate

Write a note equation to show how much chocolate is eaten by Henry, Quincy, and Doreen.

                    +   =

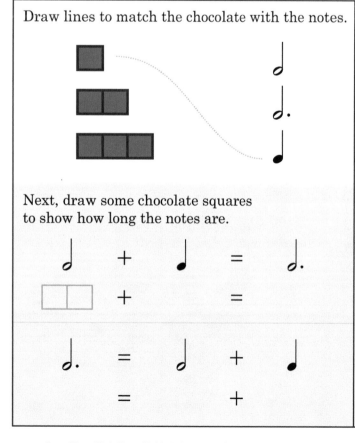

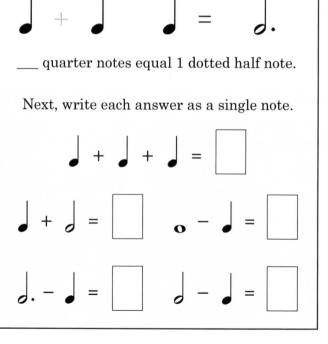

Dot Time

Draw bar lines.
Number the beats.

Next, write half notes or dotted half notes to complete each bar.

Include some ledger notes.

Quarter Notes *Walk*. Eighth Notes RUN.

Quarter notes usually go at a medium walking speed.

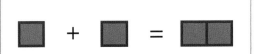

This chocolate equation reminds us that 2 quarter notes are as long as 1 h_____ note.

Trace these notes. Write a + and = sign to make a note equation.

Half notes go slower, like slow skating.

Eighth notes are faster, like a running bird.

Two eighth notes together get one quarter note beat.

Eighth notes have a flag, a stem, and a filled-in head.

Trace the arrows.

Two eighth notes last as long as ___ quarter note.

One eighth note is h_____ as long as 1 quarter note.

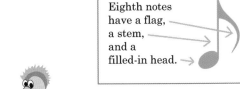

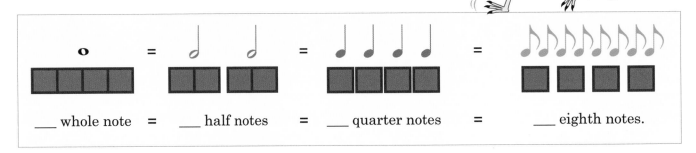

___ whole note = ___ half notes = ___ quarter notes = ___ eighth notes.

Answer with a single note.

♪ + ♪ = ☐

♪ + ♪ + ♪ + ♪ + ♪ + ♪ + ♪ + ♪ = ☐

♪ + ♪ + ♪ + ♪ = ☐

♪ + ♪ + ♪ + ♪ + ♪ + ♪ + ♩ = ☐

♪ + ♪ + ♩ = ☐

♪ + ♪ + ♪ + ♪ + ♩ = ☐

Doctor Mozart Music Theory Workbook, Level 2A.   © MMVIII, MMXV Machiko and Paul Christopher Musgrave.   Published by April Avenue Music.   www.DoctorMozart.com

2 Eighth Notes = 1 Quarter Note

Trace:

Two _____ notes are as long as one quarter note.

Answer with a single note:

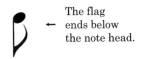

Tap these eighth notes with your right hand while you tap the quarter notes with your left. Count aloud.

Flags and Beams

When the stem points up, the flag ends *above* the note head.

The flag ← ends above the note head.

Trace. Draw the missing stems and flags.

When the stem points down, the flag ends *below* the note head.

The flag ← ends below the note head.

Trace. Draw the missing stems and flags.

Trace these notes. Some eighth notes have flags. Others are connected by beams.

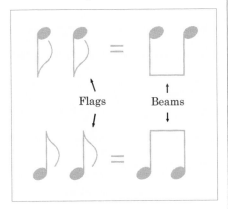

Flags Beams

Flags are always written to the right of the note stem.

Below, draw beams across each group of four notes. If *most* of the stems would normally point up, then *all* the stems should point up when joined by a beam.*

Number the beats.

1 &

1 &

---

*What if half of the notes would normally point up, and the other half would point down? Then follow the stem direction of the note that is furthest from the middle line.

Doctor Mozart Music Theory Workbook, Level 2A. © MMVIII, MMXV Machiko and Paul Christopher Musgrave. Published by April Avenue Music. www.DoctorMozart.com

Meter and Accents

Meter is the number of beats in each bar.

Duple meter means ___ beats in each bar.
Triple meter means ___ beats per bar.
Quadruple meter means ___ beats per bar.

The **top** number of the time signature tells you whether the meter is

d_____ (e.g. **2**/4 time), or

_____ (e.g. **3**/4 time), or

_____ (e.g. **4**/4 time).

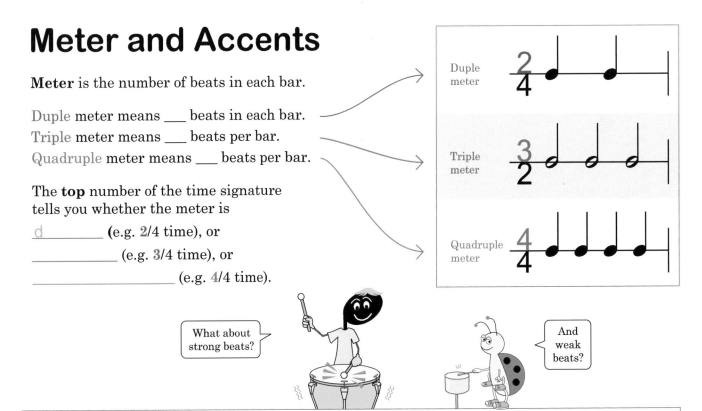

What about strong beats?

And weak beats?

The first beat of each bar is often the strongest. In **quadruple** meter, the third beat is also accented, but more softly. Here, write an accent on the *first* and *third* beat of each bar.

Quadruple meter

1st half of the bar   2nd half of the bar

Quadruple meter

Tap and count.

Number the beats.

| Primary accent | Secondary accent | Primary accent | Secondary accent | Primary accent | Secondary accent |

The ___p_____ accent is on the first beat. The _____ accent is on the third beat.
Secondary accents occur halfway through each bar in __q_____ meter.

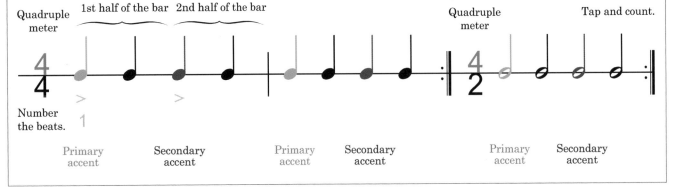

The weakest notes of all are the ones *between* beats. We count them with words like *and,* or *potato,* or *necessary,* or anything that fits. Here, tap and count, using the words shown.

weakest   weakest   weakest   weakest   weakest

1 & 2 & 3 & 4 &   1 & 2 & 3 &
1 & 2 & 3 - po - ta - to 4 - po - ta - to   1 & 2 & 3 - po - ta - to

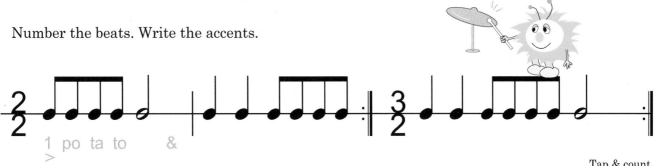

Eighth Note Rhythm Fun

Trace the gray notes. Write eighth notes to complete each bar.

$\frac{4}{4}$

1   2   &

Number the beats.   Write the primary and secondary accents.   Tap, hands together

Triple meter.

There are no secondary accents in triple or duple meter.

$\frac{3}{4}$

&   &

Next, do the same as above, but write *1 potato, 2 potato* to count the beats.

$\frac{2}{2}$

1 - po - ta - to

Number the beats. Write the accents.

$\frac{2}{2}$

1 po ta to   &

$\frac{3}{2}$

Tap & count.

Doctor Mozart Music Theory Workbook, Level 2A.   © MMVIII, MMXV Machiko and Paul Christopher Musgrave.   Published by April Avenue Music.   www.DoctorMozart.com

22

Draw the bar lines.
Name the notes.

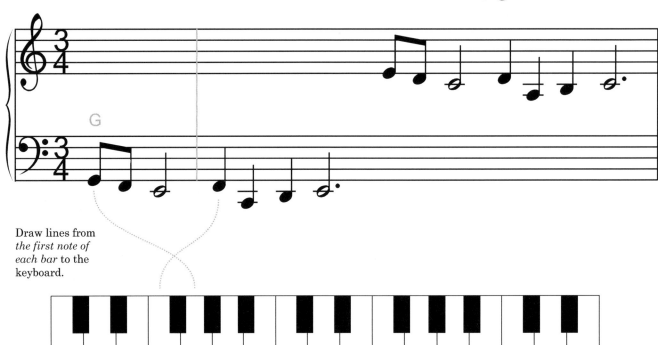

Draw lines from *the first note of each bar* to the keyboard.

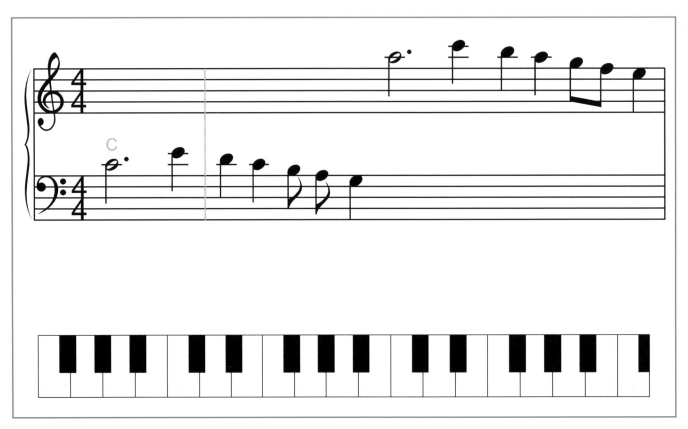

Doctor Mozart Music Theory Workbook, Level 2A.   © MMVIII, MMXV Machiko and Paul Christopher Musgrave.   Published by April Avenue Music.   www.DoctorMozart.com

RHYTHM ON THE GRAND STAFF

Fill each bar with notes – in both staffs.

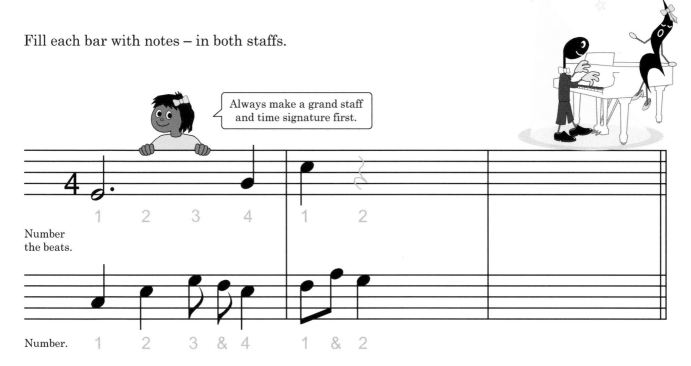

Always make a grand staff and time signature first.

Number the beats.

Number.

Include some ledger notes, eighth notes, dotted half notes, and quarter rests.

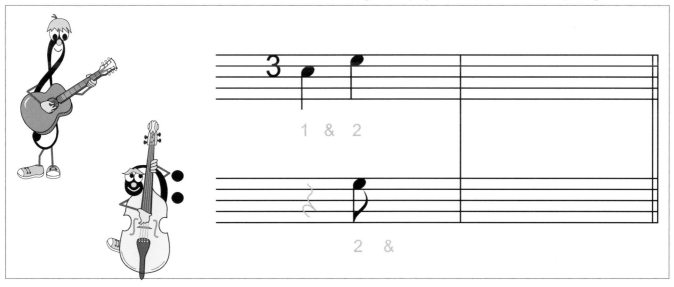

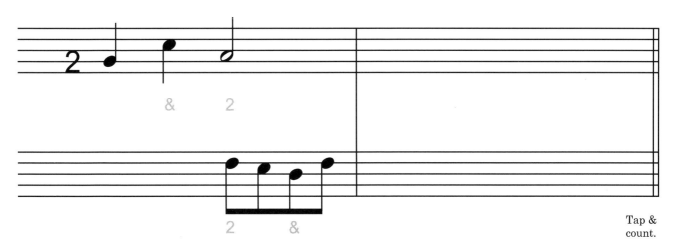

Tap & count.

Chromatic?

For each pair of notes, name the white key first. Then use the *same* letter to name the black key.

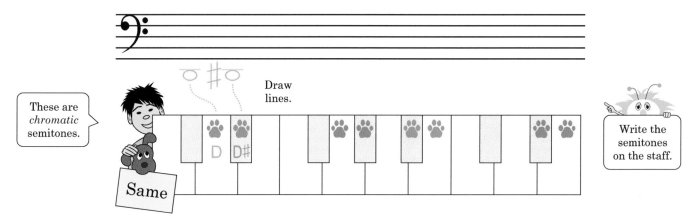

C and C# make a *chromatic* semitone, because they are both named with the *same* alphabet letter. C and C# are a c_____ semitone.

Or Diatonic?

This time, use two *different* letters to name each pair of notes.

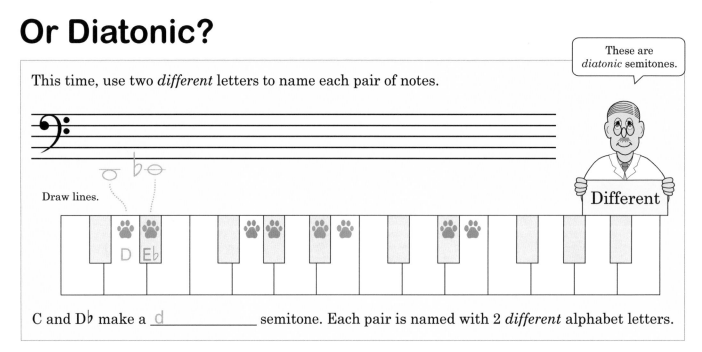

C and D♭ make a d_____ semitone. Each pair is named with 2 *different* alphabet letters.

Next, look below the keyboard to see whether each semitone is diatonic or chromatic.
Name the paw print keys. Write the semitones on the staff.

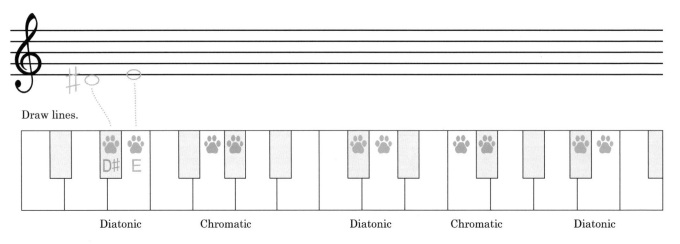

CHROMATIC AND DIATONIC

Chromatic: Same names

Diatonic: Different names

After each printed note, write a note that is a semitone *higher*.

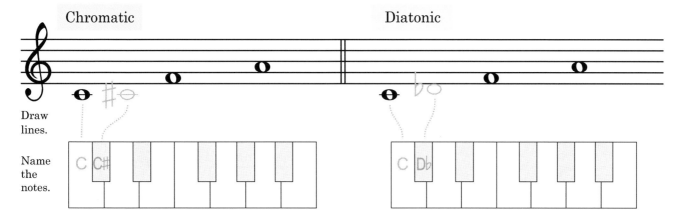

How to remember which is which: **Diatonic** and **Different** both start with **D**.

After each printed note, write a note that is a semitone *lower*. Draw lines. Name the notes.

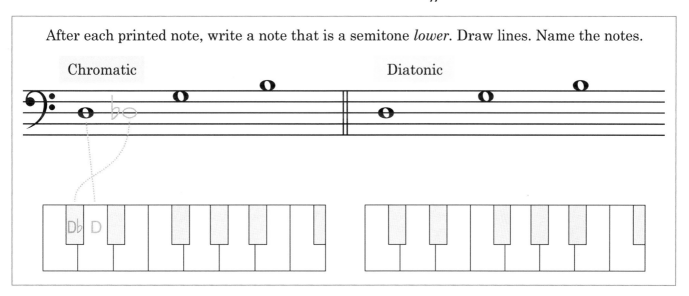

Look at the words below this keyboard. Name the paw print keys. Write the semitones on the staff.

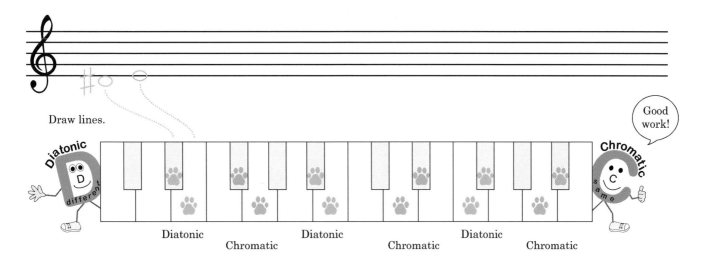

Doctor Mozart Music Theory Workbook, Level 2A.   © MMVIII, MMXV Machiko and Paul Christopher Musgrave.   Published by April Avenue Music.   www.DoctorMozart.com

ENHARMONIC Notes

Write each black key two different ways on the staff. Name the notes.

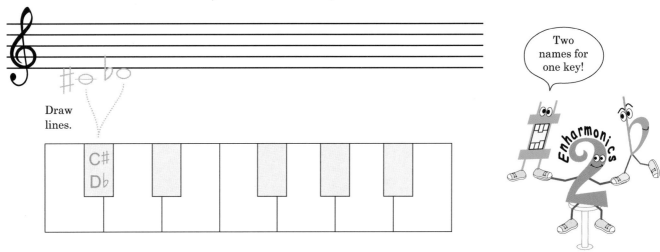

Draw lines.

C#
Db

Two names for one key!

Enharmonic equivalent is another way of saying enharmonic note. D# and E♭ are enharmonic equivalents. C# and D♭ are also _____ _____.

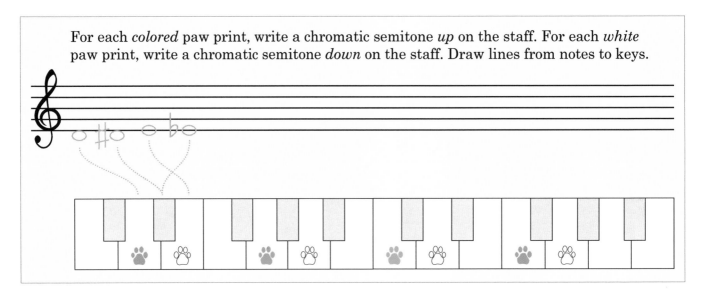

For each *colored* paw print, write a chromatic semitone *up* on the staff. For each *white* paw print, write a chromatic semitone *down* on the staff. Draw lines from notes to keys.

Write 5 pairs of enharmonic equivalent notes. Draw lines from notes to keys.

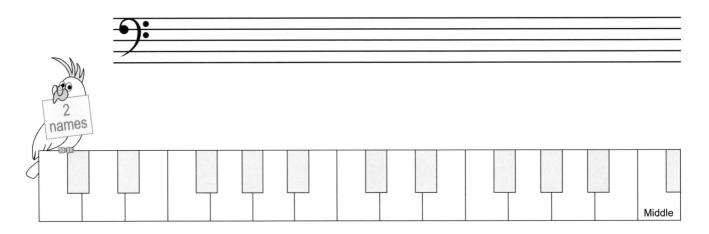

2 names

Middle

2 Half Steps = 1 Whole Step

Draw an arrow from each *left* paw print to the cat's face.
Then draw an arrow from each cat's face to the *right* paw
print. Mark each whole step with a square bracket.

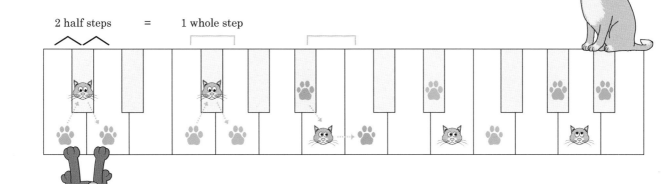

2 half steps   =   1 whole step

Each time Doctor Mozart played a whole
step, how many cats did he pass? ____
Of the whole steps he played, how many
have one white key and one black key? ____
How many have two white keys? ____
How many have two black keys? ____
One semitone = one _h_____ step.
One whole tone = one _w_____ step.

Whole steps are also
known as whole tones.

Use these
signs to show
whole steps and
half steps.

⌐┘	Square brackets for whole steps
∨	V brackets for half steps

Draw an arrow from each *left* paw print to the note
that is a whole step *higher*. Draw square brackets.

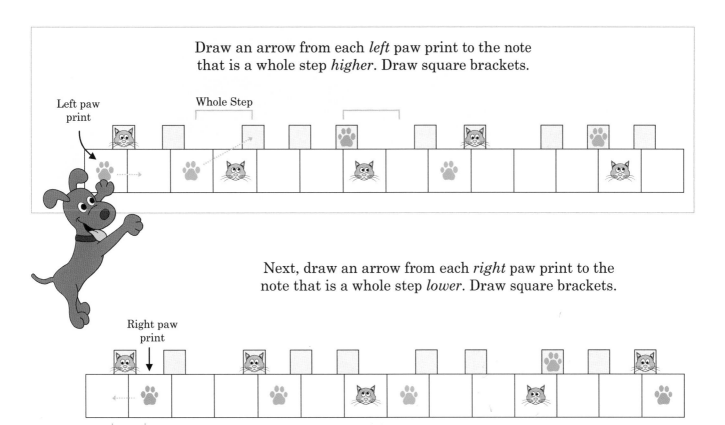

Left paw print

Whole Step

Right paw print

Next, draw an arrow from each *right* paw print to the
note that is a whole step *lower*. Draw square brackets.

Whole Steps Span Neighboring Letters

Circle all the pairs of letters that are right beside each other on the keyboard.

A C D G A D E G B D G A C E F A B F G D

The letters you circled are *neighboring* letters.

Always name whole steps with 2 *neighboring* letters.

For each paw print pair, name the white key first. Then use a *neighboring* letter to name the black key. Write each whole step on the staff.

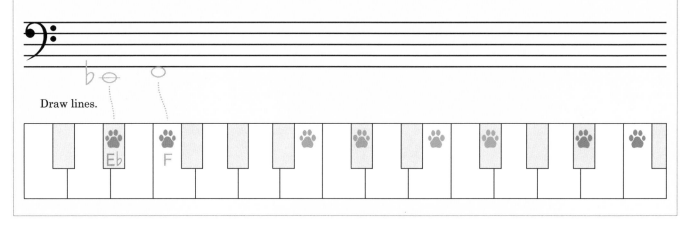

Whole steps made with 2 black keys can be named two ways. For each of these note pairs, write the whole step 2 different ways on the staff. Draw lines.

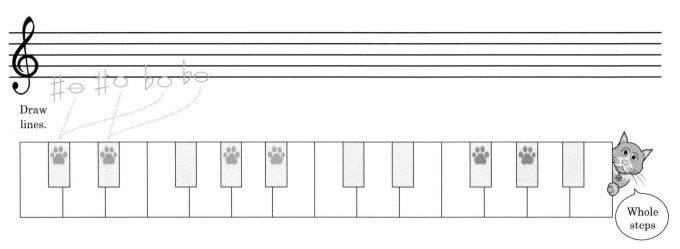

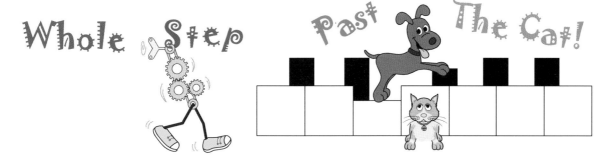

Write these whole steps on the staff. Use neighboring letters.

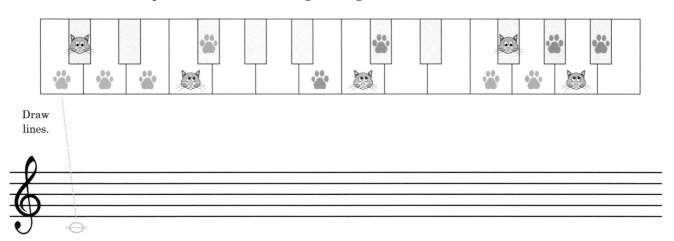

Draw lines.

Doctor Mozart wants to play whole steps that span each cat. Name the notes he should play. Always use two *neighboring* letter names.

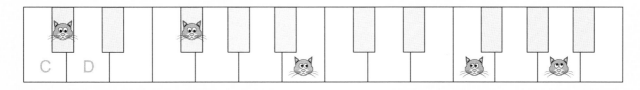

C   D

Above, how many whole steps have two white keys? _____ How many have

two black keys? _____ How many have a white key and a black key? _____

Circle any paw print pairs that make a whole step. Use neighboring letters to name them.

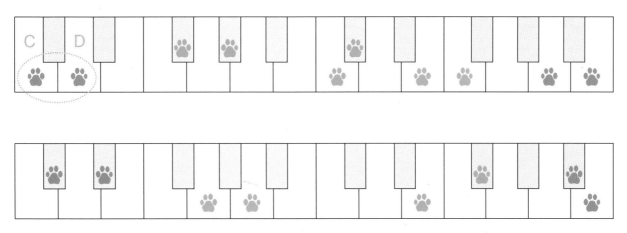

C   D

Doctor Mozart Music Theory Workbook, Level 2A.   © MMVIII, MMXV Machiko and Paul Christopher Musgrave.   Published by April Avenue Music.   www.DoctorMozart.com

Paw Print Practice

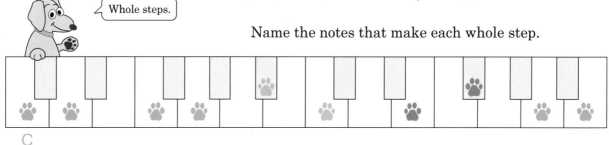

Name the notes that make each whole step.

Next, draw lines to match the meanings.

- Semitone   ● Whole step   ● The smallest distance between two keys on the keyboard
- Whole tone   ● Half step   ● A distance equal to two half steps

Name the whole steps. Write them on the staff.

Put a check mark beside each answer that is true. Put an X beside any answer that is false.

A whole step can have
- Two white keys ✓
- Two black keys
- A white key and a black key

A half step can have
- Two white keys
- Two black keys
- A white key and a black key

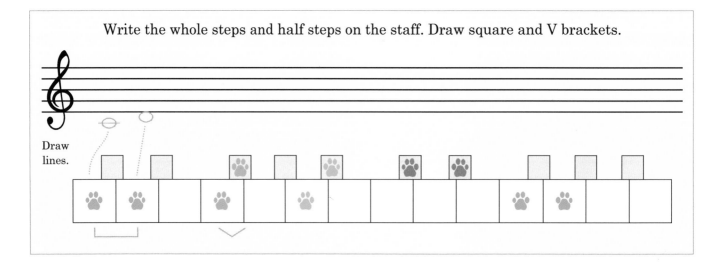

Write the whole steps and half steps on the staff. Draw square and V brackets.

Dots & Flags EXERCISE

Write one note in each box.

Write one note in each blank space. Number the beats. Tap and count.

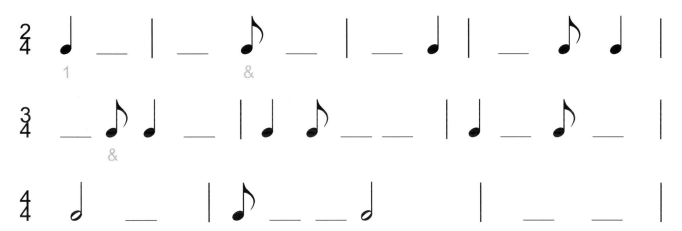

Each chocolate square equals one quarter note.
Write the *top* number for each time signature.

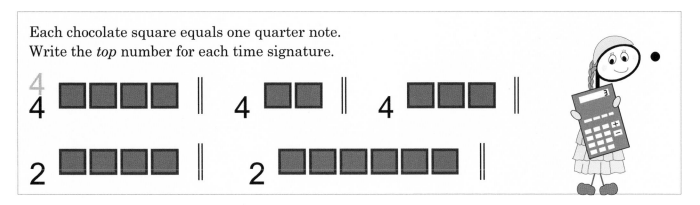

Write a treble clef and a time signature. Fill some bars with any notes you like. Number the beats.

Include some eighth notes, dotted half notes, staccato quarter notes, ledger notes, and accidentals.

Doctor Mozart Music Theory Workbook, Level 2A.   © MMVIII, MMXV Machiko and Paul Christopher Musgrave.   Published by April Avenue Music.   www.DoctorMozart.com

The C Major Scale

Trace the Roman numerals and the brackets. The Roman numerals are colored to show two *tetrachords*.

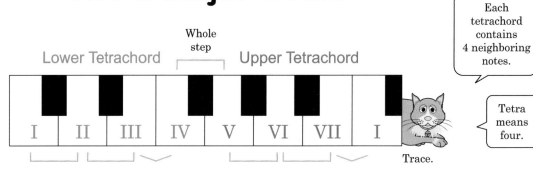

Each tetrachord contains ____ neighboring notes.

Every **major scale** contains 2 tetrachords. Trace the brackets on this car.

Notice the _____ step between the two tetrachords.

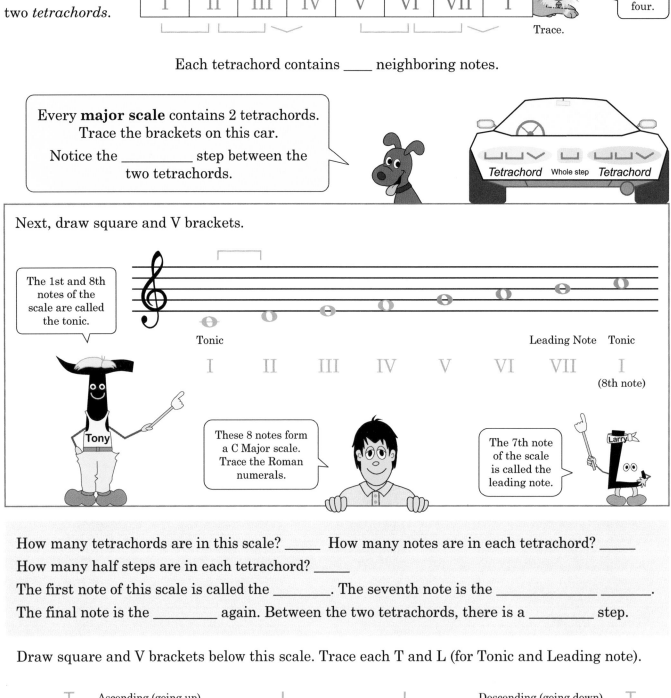

Next, draw square and V brackets.

The 1st and 8th notes of the scale are called the tonic.

These 8 notes form a C Major scale. Trace the Roman numerals.

The 7th note of the scale is called the leading note.

How many tetrachords are in this scale? _____ How many notes are in each tetrachord? _____
How many half steps are in each tetrachord? _____
The first note of this scale is called the _____. The seventh note is the _____ _____.
The final note is the _____ again. Between the two tetrachords, there is a _____ step.

Draw square and V brackets below this scale. Trace each T and L (for Tonic and Leading note).

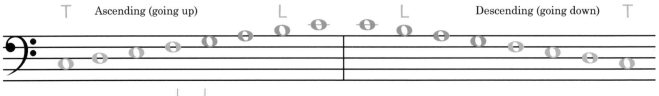

The G Major Scale

Next, write the G major key signature. Write a G major scale, ascending and descending.

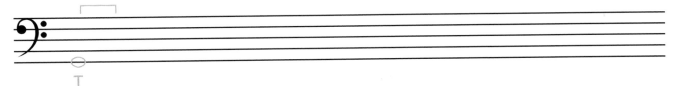

Draw brackets. Mark the tonic and the leading note.

Doctor Mozart Music Theory Workbook, Level 2A.   © MMVIII, MMXV Machiko and Paul Christopher Musgrave.   Published by April Avenue Music.   www.DoctorMozart.com

The F Major Scale

The F major scale has a black key: B♭

Complete the Roman numerals.

Draw square and V brackets.

IV

I   III   V   VII   I

Draw lines.

Circle the tonic and leading notes

Which key is black? _____
Is it the leading note? _____

Name and number the keys that form the F major scale. Draw brackets.

I
F

Write the scale.

Draw lines.

T

Write the scale on the staff. Mark the tonic and leading notes.

Next, write the F major key signature. Write an F major scale, ascending and descending.

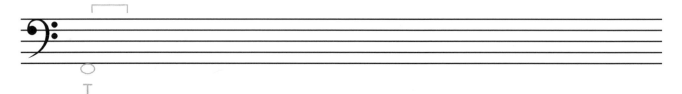

T

Draw brackets. Mark the tonic and leading notes.

Doctor Mozart Music Theory Workbook, Level 2A.   © MMVIII, MMXV Machiko and Paul Christopher Musgrave.   Published by April Avenue Music.   www.DoctorMozart.com

GRAND STAFF LEDGER NOTES REVIEW

Trace and name each note.

Connect the notes that have the same name.

A

Draw lines.

Ledger Note

Write all the white key ledger notes you have learned.

Draw lines.

Make a grand staff. For each letter, write a note near middle C – two different ways.

A   E   C   D   B

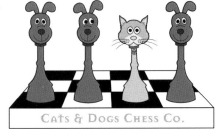

Half Step Whole Step Quiz

Name the whole steps and half steps.
Write square and V brackets.

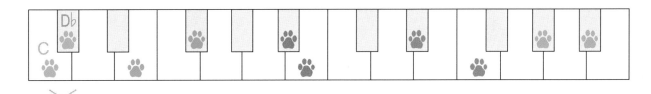

Find a *half* step *above* each paw print, and mark that note with a letter H – for *half* step.
Find a *whole* step *above* each paw print, and mark that note with a letter W – for *whole* step.

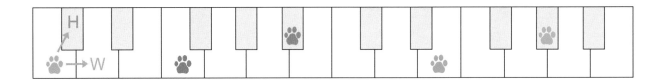

Find a *half* step *below* each paw print, and mark that note with a letter H.
Find a *whole* step *below* each paw print, and mark that note with a letter W.

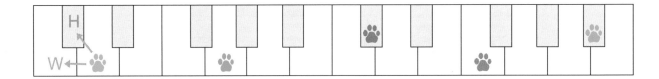

Mark each half step with a V bracket. Mark each whole step with a square bracket.

Draw
lines.

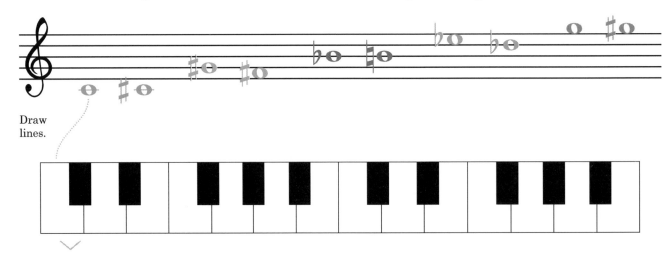

Doctor Mozart Music Theory Workbook, Level 2A.   © MMVIII, MMXV Machiko and Paul Christopher Musgrave.   Published by April Avenue Music.   www.DoctorMozart.com

Time & Tetrachord

Write one note in each empty space.

Write a G major scale ascending and descending. Draw brackets. Mark the tonic and leading notes.

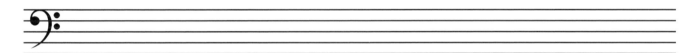

Write an F major scale going up and down. Draw brackets. Mark the tonic and leading notes.

Write an *eighth note* or a *quarter rest* or a *half rest* in each box. Number the beats.

E✗PERT Review

Write the correct clef on each staff to make
semitones that contain only white keys.

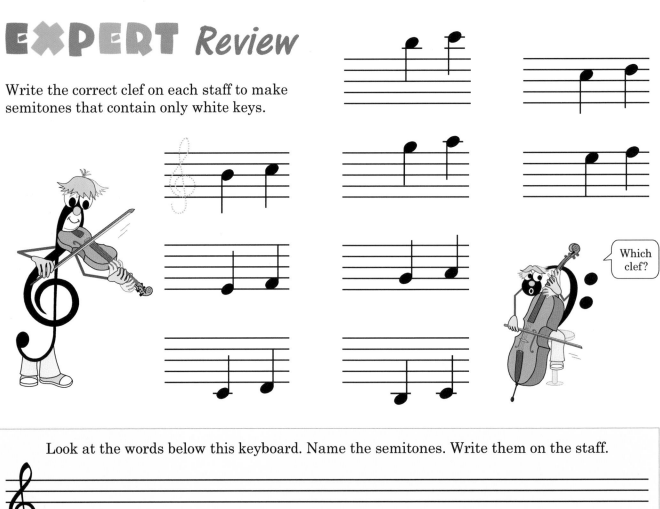

Which
clef?

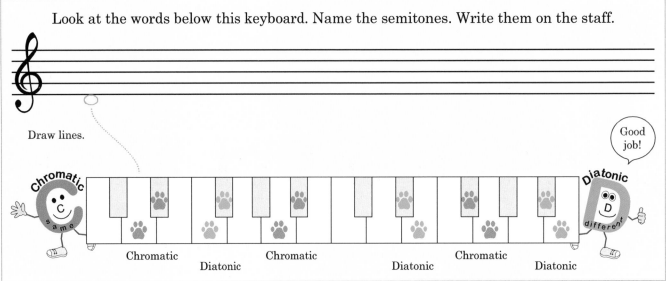

Look at the words below this keyboard. Name the semitones. Write them on the staff.

Draw lines.

Good
job!

Chromatic   Chromatic   Chromatic
        Diatonic   Diatonic   Diatonic

Make a grand staff and time signature. Fill some bars with notes. Number the beats.

Include quarter and half rests, eighth notes, dotted half notes, ledger notes, accidentals,
enharmonic equivalents, dynamics marks, and diatonic and chromatic semitones.

Doctor Mozart Music Theory Workbook, Level 2A.   © MMVIII, MMXV Machiko and Paul Christopher Musgrave.   Published by April Avenue Music.   www.DoctorMozart.com

Certificate of Achievement

_____
Student name

Now that you have completed
Doctor Mozart Music Theory
Level 2A, you are
ready for Level 2B.

Teacher _____

Date _____

Dr. Mozart

Now you
know about
ledger notes,
whole steps,
and three
major scales.

You know
about time
signatures,
dotted half
notes, and
eighth notes.

See you in
Level 2B!

In-Depth Piano Theory Fun for
Children's Music Lessons and Home Schooling.

2B

Doctor Mozart

Music Theory Workbook

It's fun!

It's in-depth.

Level 2B

Created by Machiko and Paul Christopher Musgrave

CPSIA information can be obtained
at www.ICGtesting.com
Printed in the USA
LVIC061516150720
660762LV00004B/114